FASHION TRENDS: LONDON LOOK OF T

PLEASE USE COLORED PENCILS!!

Introducing Jordan Parker
Fashion Forecaster Extraordinaire

COVER BY BRITTANY MORGANTI

PREFACE
By Leigh Rudd

Hi Coloring Book Fashionistas! Take out your colored pencils … summon your creative self … and relax with "Fashion Trends: the London Look".

Wow! This is great. For many years I've wanted to tell my story of life as a fashion forecaster and finally … here it is. It's a very personal venture and I hope you enjoy it as much as I have in creating it and my character **Jordan Parker.**

Why talk about it now? Over the years I have met hundreds of young men and women who expressed interest in exploring fashion careers and specifically in Fashion Forecasting. One of my goals is to reach out to them. Another objective is to reach fashion enthusiasts of all ages who are smitten with the 60's era which brought us such legends as: The Beatles, Rolling Stones, the Kinks: and Mary Quant, models Twiggy and Jean Shrimpton and all the famous boutiques on the King's Road that still make me smile. And I can't forget the "boomers" and older who want to reminisce about their own fun in the 60's. Welcome!

So welcome to my graphic read-along story where you can explore a world of fashion coloring. I wanted this coloring book it to be value-packed, with tons and tons of drawings to color … and it is jammed-packed with two hundred opportunities to color! Furthermore the sketches and story depict step-by-step advice – a guidebook - on what you need to become a fashion forecaster should that interest you. *Relax. Let me be your guide.*

So here is my newest project: **Jordan Parker.**

This book is dedicated to my two granddaughters Ashley and Riley.

MY "WILD CHILD" LIFE IN LONDON
By Jordan Parker

Hi young fashionistas! Welcome to Chelsea, London 1967-68 ... the fashion mecca of the world! Come relax and meditate. Allow me to tell you the story of my early days as a Fashion Forecaster ... and how I established a forecasting operating system so I could eventually have a fashion career and a company. Get out your coloring pencils and join me. Thanks!

I am so lucky! I live right in the center of Chelsea, in a quaint 1600's house just off the King's Road with my best friend Malcolm. We are just steps away from the most happening boutiques, restaurants, clubs, pubs and coffee bars ... each with its own crazy vibe.

My family calls me a wild child. Can you imagine? Well perhaps it's a tad true since the "Chelsea Set" of which I am a member is mostly hard-partying 20-ish age kids who are movers and shakers: designers, musicians and artists. Yes there are a ton of parties ... five a night on Fridays. And there's the Annabel's Club, a posh dine-and-dance spot for royals and celebrities. But let me be clear. We are all ... bar none ... young creatives working hard in the world of innovation. And, of course, we are devoted to becoming successful in our craft.

THE MAGIC OF CHELSEA IN THE 60'S

There's a magic here as if something's in the air. The "something" is attitude ... artistic, outrageous, confident and experimental. Anything and everything goes in Chelsea. Therefore, fashion is inherently unique and creative. Obviously you can wear anything and nothing is judged ... it's all very egalitarian. You could wear flowerpots on your head and everyone would just consider it a new hat trend! We all wear smoking hot fashion fads designed by wild and immensely talented young designer-retailers who live here. The vibes are everywhere, and it's a contagious energy. It's "magic". Part of the vibes come from the many hot spots here in Chelsea. They offer every type of entertainment you could ever want ... from breakfast to midnight clubbing. And by coincidence the best ones are all five minutes from my house. Am I lucky or what?

This morning I met a friend at **Picasso Coffee Bar** and said hello to David Hemmings the actor from the film Blow-Up. He's a regular and always friendly. One of my lunch favorites is **The Chelsea Kitchen.** It's not fancy or expensive but serves fresh home-made food. Yummy. The Rolling Stones crowd are often there as well as the famous soccer player George Best.

Then I popped up the road to **Antiquarius** to wander through art dealers' stalls. I was looking for an art nouveau or deco perfume bottle and didn't find one so I ran to the other end of the King's Road to explore the **Chelsea Antique Market:** a conglomeration of shops and stalls. I went immediately to Pattie Boyd's art nouveau stall called **Juniper.** I found exactly what I needed. She's the English model and wife of The Beatle George Harrison. Very friendly local girl.

Last night we all went to the members-only **Club dell' Artusa**. John Lennon was there with Yoko Ono, and so were David Bailey and Twiggy. Another favorite local club is **The Pheasantry** located in an historic Georgian building. You go downstairs to the night club, and by the way Eric Clapton is a resident upstairs. Often Malcolm and I will go across the road to **The Markham Arms Pub** where Mary Quant and her husband can often be found at night nattering with friends. Of course her boutique **Bazaar** is on the corner of Markham Square. And Friday night is always a string of parties ... then off to meet friends at the members-only **Annabel's Club**. Finally ... In Chelsea we have a fun-filled tradition of parading up and down the King's Road called the "Saturday Fashion Parade;" all gorgeous young fashionistas and peacock males in daring outfits. It's a people-watching frenzy! So much FUN! But I'm not just an empty-headed girl. I also love to explore art galleries, research museums and look for treasures in antique markets. And I even read history books for background on cultural changes. For now I'm just staying in the moment and figuring it out as I go along.

Chelsea is an affluent area of southwest London, mostly within the Royal Borough of Kensington and Chelsea, a two-mile stretch that goes from Sloan Square to the up-and-coming World's End. Chelsea became "a lifestyle" in the 1960's for the young and innovative who flocked there. New concepts of music, design, and marketing emerged and impacted the world of fashion and the arts and changed entire industries and generated billions of pounds and dollars for those involved.

HOME SWEET HOME! WELCOME!

To get on with the story this impressive door is the entryway to my quaint house and life with my best friend and flat-mate Malcolm, a phenome fashion illustrator. I'm pretty out-going and he's the opposite so we're a good team. He could clean up with free-lance but is too shy to take his portfolio around. So I sometimes go with him, but we always end up in an argument because he claims I talk about fashion trends that no one understands. Like the Fall of Rome ... one of my favorites. Honestly!

When I'm not at the museums, antique markets, clubs, coffee bars and boutiques ... my house is where I play fashion dress-up with Malcolm ... like children.

I painted my door a very special red: the color of Revlon's FIRE AND ICE lipstick. I want to make sure that you can spot our door from way down the street! But please free to color the door with whatever shade moves you.

Color is a meaningful (but fun) business, with each hue giving off an emotional meaning. You get vibes and you give out vibes depending on the color. The color red, for example, is vibrant and energetic ... just like me!

So come on in and enter my world where I spend my nights (when I'm not at Annabel's) playing with my fashion inspiration — bolts of fabric, on-the-street photos, color palettes and vintage fashion from the masters — it's all here.

I'm in-and-out of this red door a hundred times a day, always bringing home a new something or other for my collection of inspirations. I'm five minutes on foot from the "I'm fabulous" attitude of the King's Road. And I just got home from Quorum, the Ossie Clark boutique around the corner where I bought a printed chiffon Ossie dress; ankle-length and fluid. Marvelous babe!

MY QUAINT HOUSE

As I've said ... our charming house is perfect for a busy lifestyle so near the restaurants and clubs ... and of course the boutiques. I'm in and out a hundred times a day. Malcolm is usually home at his drawing board doing work for Selfridge's.

The house is spacious, with three bedrooms and a sweet garden in back. But naturally the sun rarely comes out, and when it peeks out, we practically trample each other to get outside. We each have our own bedrooms which is good because Malcolm is neat-obsessive and mine is cluttered with fabric swatches and magazines. "It is authentic, not changed much from the 1600's! The fridge is so tiny that a tin of sweets fills it up. There's no heat or air conditioning. But there's a tiny contraption in my bedroom where I put in a shilling and a bit of heat comes out ... but only for a few minutes. It must be from the 17th century!

The sitting room is decorated in what is called "shabby genteel" style, which means draperies, and furniture are worn and faded. It's funny that shabby genteel became a trendy look! But for one ... shiny, spanking new and modern home decor in England is considered terribly bad taste.

By the way, my Chelsea neighbors are Mary Quant, Mick Jagger, Twiggy, Pattie Boyd, Eric Clapton, the Duchess of Cambridge, Judy Garland, Ava Gardner and Sir Laurence Olivier ... just to name a few. We are used to seeing celebrities around town so they just merge in with the locals.

MY BEDROOM: THE FASHION LAB

My room is a cluttered mess of fashion ideas!   But brilliant ones! And Malcolm (the perfectionist) ... well ... it makes him a total lunatic!! My room is wall-to-wall sketchpads, colors, textures, swaths of fabrics, fashion photos and drawings. Okay, I admit it's untidy. But I consider it a fashion laboratory of inspirational supplies like fabrics and vintage photos that fuel my design concepts.

My best stuff, of course, is stapled, pinned, glued and tacked up on the walls. And one of the things I love most is selecting colors from photos of magnificent exotic birds I see in National Geographic. I combine these colors in prints I design. There's nothing like the beauty of jungle animals.

I have a basket full of bolts of fabric. When I'm obsessed with the look of a certain fabric I buy the entire bolt. Most of the time I can only afford bits of fabric, maybe a half-yard that I've negotiated off a vendor at the Portobello Antique Market.

Even my floor is cluttered! I have piles of stuff like seed pearls from the 1920's, glass buttons from the 1930's, and trims like military braids, and glitzy sequins from ballroom competitions. And my drawers are full of feathers and veils for the cocktail hats Malcolm and I make. Malcolm nags endlessly. So I finally invested in huge Styrofoam boards to use as mood boards and smaller portable ones. I study them when I meditate.

I also like to read so my night table is stacked with books which have influenced me over the years, like Gone with the Wind, Alice in Wonderland and The Art of War. I tend to lie in bed and either read or write in my secret diary which I keep under my bed. Fashion requires a CIA level of secrecy don't you think?

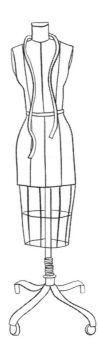

ARMOIRE ... MY COLLECTION OF VINTAGE

I am so in love with my antique armoire. When one is storing vintage art pieces of fashion design, the furniture must be stately and elegant. It needs to be a fitting piece of furniture to keep my most precious vintage dresses and accessories that date from the 1920's through the 1950's.

You probably wonder where all these clothes have come from, right? I've collected select garments and special pieces slowly and carefully since I was thirteen-years-old! Mind you I don't have tons of them. But each one is a treasure.

I especially love the clothes of French designers Madeleine Vionnet and Coco Chanel, both born in the 1800's. They were early champions of the female body and that is evident in their designs from the 1920's to the 1950's. Both designers addressed a liberated style of dressing. They exhibited an attitude of the empowered modern woman.

Armoire is a "wardrobe" cupboard. In the pre built-in closet days, a freestanding cabinet was necessary. Mine has bi-parting cabinet doors.

MAGIC OF THE KICK-ASS LONDON BOUTIQUES

Shops here are like a theatre stage, a Hollywood movie showcasing dramatic and daring "fashion looks" from tip to toe Which reflect the distinctive personality of its founder-retailer-designer. One of the most eclectic shops is my favorite, Granny Takes a Trip, in World's End. It opened a couple of years ago and is bringing this part of town (World's End) to life. The founders are collectors of vintage clothing but they update them for the 60's with expert tailoring. The clothing stock is a crazy mish-mash of the colorful and unique, hippie with an LSD spin, all influenced by Aubrey Beardsley and art nouveau. But MOST FABULOUS is their huge mural; a pop art painting on the shop front of Jean Harlow, the 1920's movie star. And, of course, there's Mary Quant's iconic shop **Bazaar** where she showcases her revolutionary mini-skirt Chelsea look in 1960. Other designers and retailers followed. She also started the trend of designing and selling affordable clothing. Her windows are a big talking point, re-styled almost once a week. She takes window dressing to a new high with extraordinary themes and accessories. Then there is Quorum with a totally different, more elegant and exclusive look where the designer **Ossie Clark's** dresses are featured. And his wife, **Celia Birtwell**, designs the most amazing dress prints. Then there's the **BIBA** boutique, another favorite. It is a "total look"; for example, the dark and decadent Art Deco theme of founder-designer **Barbara Hulanicki**. Down to the last ashtray, she integrates the merchandise, the interior decor, the adverts and the marketing. It is one entire statement! Other shops are: **Just Looking** with its many mirrors and ear-splitting loud music which is geared to the young customer. It is designed by the same architects who are planning a huge, multi-level store called **The Drugstore**, which is based on the one in Paris.

Here are just a few of these fabulous shops: **Dandie Fashions ... Kleptomania ... Apple Tailoring ... Blakes of Chelsea ... Guys N' Dolls** and **Hung on You.**
Enjoy the coloring!

MORE ON CHELSEA ...
FASHION ITEMS THAT DEFINE THE ERA

This is a decade that breaks with the fashion traditions of the 1950's. And of course, the clothing mirrors the social and cultural revolution of the time, as well as creating a few new popular fashion items.

- FALSE EYELASHES AND KOHL-RIMMED EYES
- PATTERNED TIGHTS WITH KNEE-LENGTH FLAT BOOTS
- MARYJANE SHOES
- WHITE GO-GO BOOTS
- TRANSPARENT BLOUSES AND DRESSES
- TEENY-TINY HOT PANTS
- TEENY MICRO MINI SKIRTS (shorter than mid-thigh)
- MINI SKIRTS — MID-THIGH
- HIPPIE MOCCASINS, LOVE BEADS, PEACE SIGNS
- DECORATED BLUE JEANS: Embroidered, stone-encrusted and painted
- FRAYED BELL BOTTOM JEANS
- FLOWING CAFTANS
- LONG MAXI COATS TO ANKLES
- NEHRU JACKETS FOR MEN AND WOMEN
- WIDER TIES FOR MEN, 5 INCHES WIDE IN CRAZY PRINTS

SUPERMODELS OF THE SWINGING SIXTIES

There are a handful of top models here in London, and they're all trendsetters who set the cultural tempo for London. And it's not just in clothing, their influence is broader and comprises where to eat, where to vacation and how to decorate.

And there are also the personal fads of the models which get picked up by the masses of young women. Examples are: the Twiggy Panda eyes and freckles and double-thick spiky eyelashes. Then there are the Penelope Tree lashes. Check them out.

I ran into **Twiggy** at Annabel's last night and thought to myself what a celebrity she has become in the past few years. Funny really … she's a stick-thin kid with big eyes and boyish hair but nevertheless she has stolen everyone's heart — I think it's her waif look of innocence. And now every girl in Britain is trying to look like Twiggy — good luck with that!

Then there's **Penelope Tree**, a society-model who is photographer David Bailey's favorite subject. I ran into them in Paris recently … just a little boutique-hopping trip for me. Penelope makes her own statement. In her case it is her white skin, moon-shaped eyes and spiky eye lashes on the lower lids.

Actually, the first supermodel here was **Jean Shrimpton** in 1960. She's called, "the face of the Swinging Sixties London." David Bailey photographed her for British Vogue in a bold spread that broke away from the prim and proper 1950's style. "The Shrimp" as she was called, was the first to make the mini-skirt popular … and she was called the "most beautiful girl in the world" by the press. Another model that helps define the look of the 60's is the exotic and fabulous 6'3" **Veruschka**. She reminds me of a magnificent, rangy jungle cat.

"YOU ARE A FASHION FORECASTER!"

What a morning this has been ... life-changing I would say. Malcolm and I were working in my room with some tulle and Lycra fabrics in bright red and black. We placed a rhinestone and seed pearl trim on the tulle, and I used words like "Dance" then "Ballroom" and "Latin Hustle". We were just playing fashion but my mind kept racing. Malcolm doodled as we talked.

Suddenly it came to me! How about "Salsa Craze." Malcolm looked at me with a huge smile. I smiled too and he began sketching in a frenzy. His drawings were marvelous, an entire collection of salsa skirts, rhumba, and tango dresses.

We were crazy with inspiration. We quickly pulled the sketches, fabrics, colors and trims together, then glued them on heavy construction paper. We taped the Salsa Craze fashion story on the wall and sat back to contemplate it. We nodded with approval. Suddenly Malcolm jumped to his feet and said,

"I know what you are! JP ... YOU'RE A FASHION FORECASTER!"

Immediately I knew he was right. A million questions went through my head like; how do I do it, is there a system or a step-by-step guide, where do I start? So we brainstormed a basic plan of action. Malcolm wrote down these words and they have changed my life forever.

Intuition ... Research ... Exploration ... Observation

COLLECTING FORECASTING SUPPLIES

I pondered Malcolm's words: Intuition ... Research ... Exploration ... Observation. I wrote about each of them for hours in my JP Diary. For starters Intuition is an asset, which luckily I have. Some call it a Sixth Sense. Some call it being a Visionary.

Then I jump into gear. OK, I thought, what supplies do I need? You'll think this is crazy but the first decision was a pair of sneakers for rushing around town. I chose my red high top sneakers. Once again they match Revlon's Fire and Ice lipstick red. And I knew I needed my camera. I photo everything I see ... on-the-street fashion, trendy spots with fabulous people, rock concerts ... well you get it.

Another question came up: how can I carry all this stuff? Should I design a huge carryall bag, big enough to carry my supplies? Maybe polka dots? I bet my best friend Rosie will help me. Then I thought immediately maybe I should make a few bags ... in different color combinations.

So if I'm a fashion forecaster ... how in the world do I display my trend ideas? I need a location where I can look at a complete Fashion Trend in one place. I'm going to need a humungous board to pin Malcolm's sketches ... a few fabric swatches and colors ... and the inspirational photos from National Geographic ... graphs for following socio-economics... and newspaper headlines. There is no end to what I need to be a forecaster. Oh dear!

First I'll get a cork foam board, maybe in a few sizes so I can pin stuff to it. I'll need to display trends.

And, of course, I have to fortify my art supplies. As you probably guessed supplies are an on-going process. I don't need to get all of it on day one. But I need to get started.

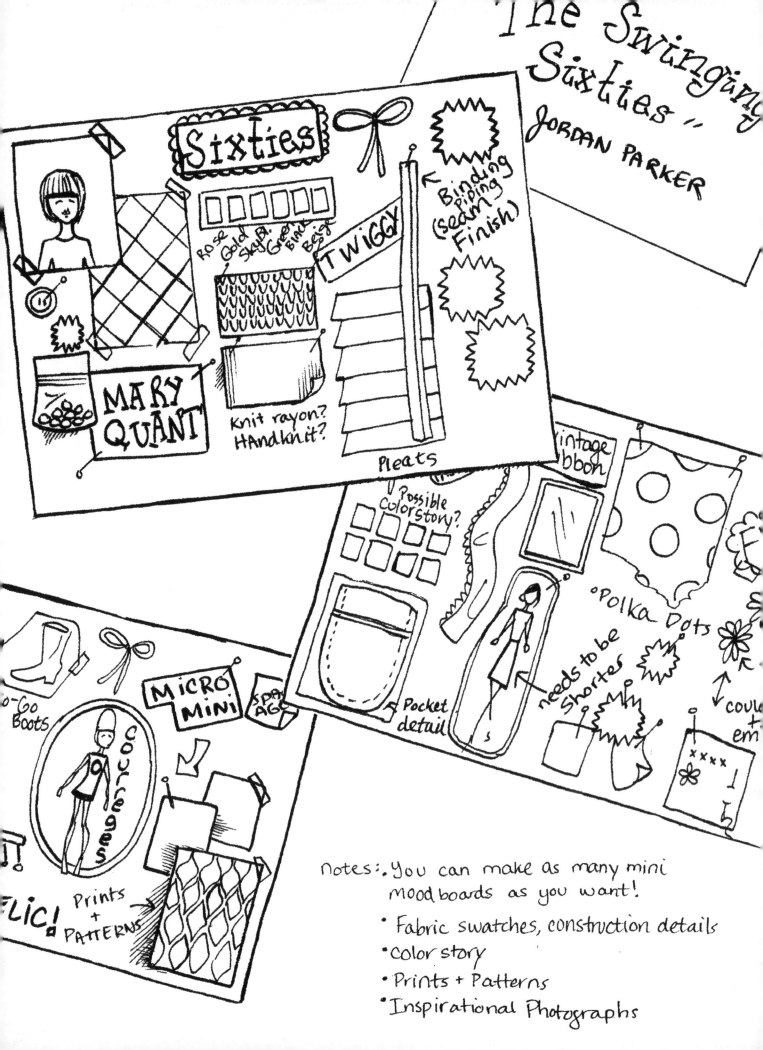

"The Swinging Sixties"

JORDAN PARKER

THE MAGIC OF COLOR

Color is magical the way it reflects our feelings and even world events. Did you know that every color in the universe contains emotion-centric messages? In fact it's been determined by science that color can influence our hormones, blood pressure and emotions. We are all influenced by color every day, whether we realize it or not. How's that for research?

Sometimes it is not the color itself, but a combination of colors. Two vibrant colors used together creates a young, sassy attitude. Neon colors used together usually give off an air of high risk and adventure. Black is often used to balance bright colors; it creates a touch of elegance in combination with the assertive point-of-view of vibrant shades.

Color can change depending on the fabric it is on. For example, pale pink is different on silk than it is on burlap. They give off different vibes so they engender different reactions.

Now that I have been dubbed a "Fashion Forecaster" by Malcolm, I feel a bit like an expert. I can share that color is always a reflection of culture and happenings. The consumer, when shopping, is influenced by color. For example, if times are tough a consumer may be attracted by brighter colors to offset anxiety.

Now in the 1960's the acid neon colors and psychedelic prints reflect the music, drugs and attitude of rebellion. Look at the influence of the hippie musical "Hair" ... one of the most influential trend setter shows of the decade.

So when I forecast a new season I instinctively take the temperature of our culture, politics, events, popular music and I tune into the customer's world. You will need a Pantone wheel to match your colors with whatever your inspiration is ... a piece of art, for example. Just slip the color wheel into your bag with your camera wherever you go.

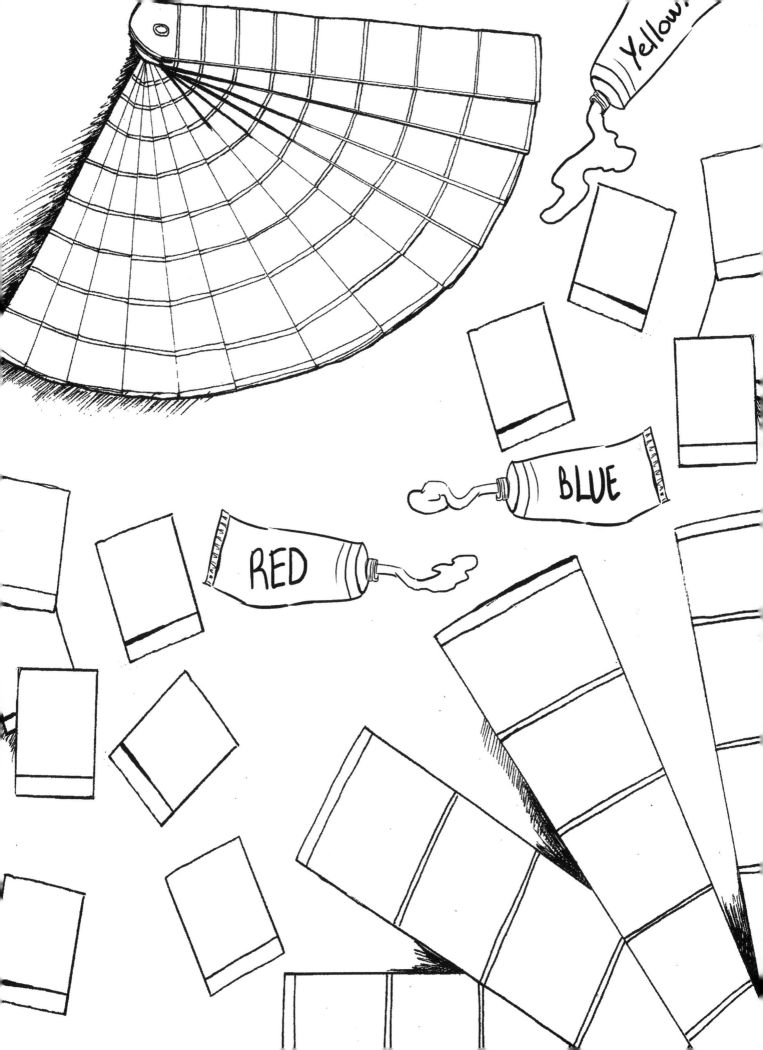

RESEARCH AS MUCH AS POSSIBLE FOR IDEAS

An important part of my research is what I call retro-hunting. I go to the Portobello Road Antique Market on most Saturday mornings, a source of amazing stimulation. I can buy at least three things for a five-pound note! My money goes far because my favorite activity of all time is to negotiate with vendors for a little Victorian brooch or an original Beardsley print or a bolt of fabric.

There are also all kinds of second-hand stalls and bric-a-brac vendors. There are even stalls for new but highly discounted clothes. And there are over a thousand vendors at Portobello ... with masses of stuff to discover. Dealers began moving into Portobello Road seventy years ago.

I usually ask Malcolm or my friend Rosie to retro-hunt with me. They always say yes because they love it too. Rose is into vintage accessories. And Malcolm searches high and low for sketchpads from some famous person usually lost under a bunch of dusty old comic books or something. And right now I'm into art nouveau mirrors and scarves. We put on old clothes and dig through antique postcards, posters, brooches and what-have-you and run around like a bunch of kids.

After that we rush home to change into something fabulous for the Saturday Parade on the King's Road. Then after that we're off to the Markham Arms Pub ... and a string of parties ... then a night at the Annabel's Club. This is how I got my wild child reputation! But now that I'm a Fashion Forecaster I have to be more serious. Or not!

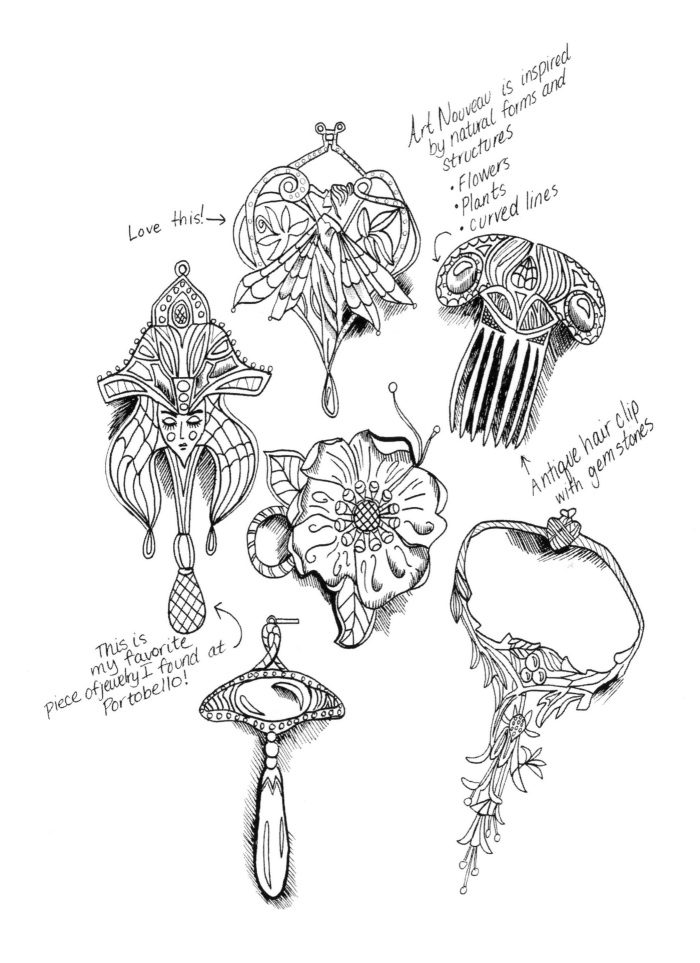

Love this! →

Art Nouveau is inspired by natural forms and structures
• Flowers
• Plants
• curved lines

Antique hair clip with gemstones

This is my favorite piece of jewelry I found at Portobello!

RESEARCH PREVIOUS ERAS

I often meditate about fashion from earlier decades because they still have a huge impact on design and tailoring. And now that I'm a Fashion Forecaster ... well ... you know the rest of the story. You could say I've developed a philosophy about fashion history. Historical design doesn't return exactly as it was; however, innovative and high-quality design will come back over and over if it is great. So I try to become familiar with designs from the 20's or 30's ... right through the 50's. In my opinion dressmaking can be like fine art and should be treasured as such. It must, of course, be superior quality in fabric and tailoring and in every aspect of the design. It must make a statement. Yes, history repeats itself even in fashion design.

And where to research you ask? I begin with a list of museums, costume exhibitions, galleries and libraries that are not too far away so I can visit and re-visit them. Now it's time to gather supplies. (1) A jot pad for tons of note-taking (2) Sketchpads for doodling (3) Colored pencils and (4) Color wheels for matching hues. (5) A giant-sized tote bag to pack it all up.

Here are a few suggestions. Spend a day at the Costume Institute at the Metropolitan Museum in New York City or the Victoria and Albert in London. Visit the libraries in fashion schools: The Fashion Institute of Technology, LIM College, The New School, Parsons and the FIDM (Fashion Institute in Los Angeles California).

Here are a few ideas to get started:
1920'S: Roaring Twenties "Flappers"
1930'S: Glamour, Femininity, midi-length skirts
1940'S: Influence of Hollywood Glamour
1950'S: Bobby Socks, Saddle Shoes, Big Skirts and Crinolines

SUPERSTAR DESIGNERS OF THE 60'S

Fashion designers reflect the culture; however, during the 60's designers increase the impact ... and often WERE the trend. Therefore ... the Swinging Sixties in London are a perfect back-drop for cutting edge and rebellious fashion.

Swinging London is a term for the reckless, fun-loving scene flourishing; a throwback to the rebellious 1920's. Both decades adopted, for example, an innocent yet naughty little girl look. Consider the "Flappers" and the "Chelsea Girls" ... both in scandalously short skirts with a devil-may-care attitude.

I must say, however, that I'm proud to be part of this new and distinct 20-ish culture that includes so many talented people. The style explosion is mainly in London; however, French designer **André Courrèges** is making a splash with his futuristic collections. Check out his fabulous white go-go boots and his own version of the mini-dress. Last year I had a summer intern job working directly with him in Paris. What an opportunity! Loved it! I was responsible for getting his clothes to the magazines ... in French mind you. Another English designer-retailer is **Barbara Hulanicki**. She founded the legendary Biba boutique. It is such a humungous success that Biba actually has its own little girl look; a tinge of decadence with jewel-tone colors and leopard prints. I think it was Barbara who said, "The Biba look' is long-legged fresh little foals with bright faces." A teenager named Anna Wintour worked there recently. And one of my personal favorites is English **designer Ossie Clark** one of the all-time "greats" who influences many other designers including Yves Saint Laurent. Ossie hit his stride a couple of years ago in 1965. The fashion press dubbed him the "King of King's Road". He is known for his muted colors and **Celia Birtwell's** dress prints. Celia is also his wife. I can be found on many days wearing a floaty ankle-length printed chiffon dress which barely skims my body. Absolutely the most comfortable dress I've ever worn.

POPULAR PRINTS AND PATTERNS

Wow!! I love prints and patterns ... everywhere and on everything. And it's so cool in London that men and women wear the same prints!

Here are a few:

ART NOUVEAU AND ART DECO "LIBERTY" PRINTS

PSYCHEDELIC: Inspired by the art of my friend Peter Max. Psychedelic shock-colors are everywhere even in traditional London.

BRIGHTLY COLORED TIE-DYE: Associated with the Hippie Look.

PAISLEY PATTERNS: Originating in India, one of the most popular designs: an intricate pattern made up of curved feather like shapes.

FLORALS: Seen everywhere. Tea rose, glazed calico with large floral patterns, art nouveau, Eastern-influence, stylized, realistic, wallpaper patterns; all sizes from miniature to oversized patterns.

GEOMETRICS: A mood of modernity with an influence of artists: Op Art Bridget Riley in black and white; also Mondrian as shown by Mary Quant, Yves St, Laurent and André Courrèges.

POP ART: Pop Art in bright colors. Patterns from young contemporary artists like Andy Warhol and Roy Lichtenstein who is a pal of mine.

CHECKERBOARD PATTERNS & GINGHAMS

EASTERN INFLUENCE: Batik patterns, paisley prints from India.

AND SO MANY OTHERS! In fact pattern and print designs are much more popular than solids for dresses, shirts, and blouses. Men like printed jackets and suits on satin and corduroy. It is a welcome change to see fashion barriers between the sexes fall away!

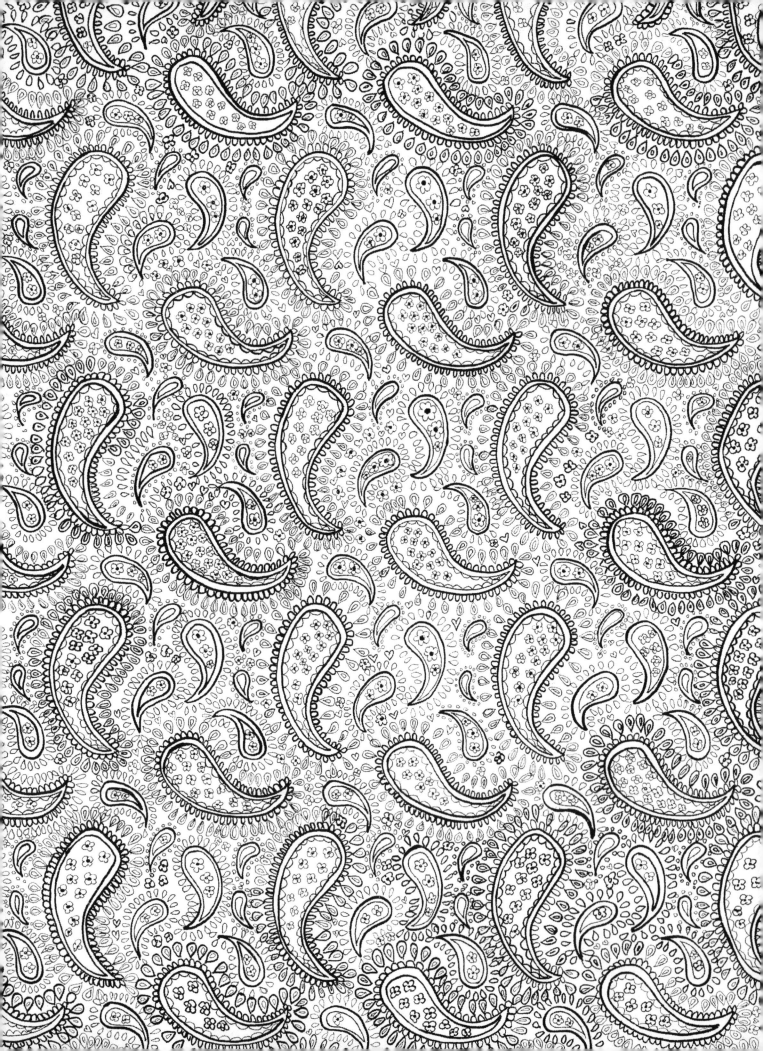

T-SHIRTS ... DAY OR EVE ... WORK OR HOME

SALSA SKIRT T-Shirts can be purchased at:
shop.spreadshirt.com/SexSells2016
On the following pages the T-shirt is shown with our Spring-Summer Trends.

Our Spring-Summer 2016 -17 FASHION TRENDS
Oversized Florals … Border Prints on Skirts … Ruffled & Tiered Skirts … Cropped Pants
… More Shredded Denim! Our Sex Sells! T-Shirt is the perfect little top for all the new
trends. It's a must-have purchase! Look at the next pages of Trends.

LOGO CONTROVERSY OF SALSA SKIRT T-SHIRTS
By Leigh Rudd

Fashion and Glamour are intertwined. So are Glamour and Sex … so are Fashion and Sex Appeal. So that's my premise … and that's why I thought it would be fun to design a "Sex Sells! T-Shirt LOGO. But there are friends and family saying, "Leigh! You can't do that! You cannot mention Sex in a nice coloring book. What if a fourteen year old were to see it?" I thought to myself, "Are you kidding? Have you watched TV recently? And besides … this coloring book for is for grown-ups."

And that is why I combined Fashion, Glamour and Sex Appeal into one T-Shirt LOGO, by the way, which portrays a fabulous "Salsa Skirt" … influenced by the Latin Hustle and Salsa Dancing.

shop.spreadshirt.com/SexSells2016

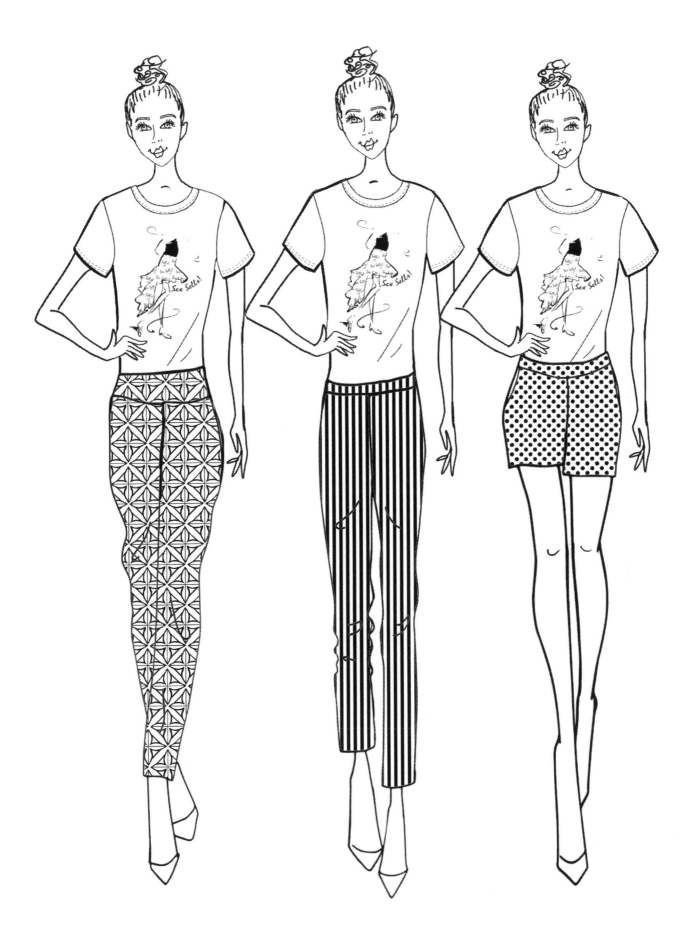

shop.spreadshirt.com/SexSells2016

shop.spreadshirt.com/SexSells2016

shop.spreadshirt.com/SexSells2016

THE FASHION TEAM

Welcome to Our World!
Thanks and Gratitude from Leigh Rudd!

Brittany Morganti: Designer – Writer - Fashion Assistant - Forecaster

My grateful thanks to my Fashion Assistant Brittany, 24, who has been by my side for the past six months working tirelessly on this coloring book with me. Not only is Brittany a multi-dimensional talent she also has a passion for going the extra mile to develop an extraordinary product. Her many talents include design, writing, and drawing ... with an instinct for marketing and branding. Above all ... she sees fashion through the lens of an explosive energy of creativity. This is a name to watch ... a girl who is going someplace. Although she is a sensitive artist ... she is also a powerful force for young women, an admirable role model. Thank you Brittany for giving me the opportunity of working with you. I feel honored to have you by my side. Thank goodness we laugh a lot. :) Right?
www.BGDfashion.com
Brittanymorganti@icloud.com

David Wolfe: Fashion Legend – Artist – Paper Doll Pioneer

A special shout-out to my dearest friend David Wolfe, a man whose talent knows no bounds. He is a legendary artist, trend-spotter, writer, fashion presenter and innovator. And now he is equally famous as a paper doll artist of vintage and movie star fashion. His work is pure artistry. David has been my colleague since 1968 when I founded IM INTERNATIONAL in London and hired David as my Creative Director. My favorite day of the week is Sunday when we talk on the phone about our favorite TV shows and funniest fashion forecasting stories. David is a genius innovator! He is a Creative Director at The Doneger Group.
www.paperdollywood.com

Randy Becker: Producer - Director –– Strategist - Coach - Master Showman

Randy is a brilliant strategist and entertainment coach ... definitely the man you want on your team as you explore your work dreams. His vision is unparalleled. His clients include writers, film makers, actors, producers and directors. Somehow Randy is always able to see around the corner; he sees the road blocks ahead and helps you solve challenges gracefully and effectively. He seems to have the answers to the What If's ... and that's half the battle. Right? He never allows his clients to give up! And I shall be forever grateful. Today his innovative screenplay competitions, coaching programs, and live events bring powerful opportunities to his many clients. Randy Becker is a 360 degree strategic thinker. Brilliant!
www.nextventertainment.com

Amanda Hallay: Creative Giant — Pop Culture Professor - Humorist

Amanda is a lifetime family friend and I feel honored to have watched her grow over the years. Professor Hallay is an author and college professor specializing in Fashion History and 20th Century Popular Culture. Spending most of her life in London and Paris, she currently lives on the Long Island coast in a home she describes as a "Kennedy Era beach house", and teaching the culture of fashion at a leading Manhattan fashion college. Her passion is teaching and I admire her for that. Anyone who has the opportunity of spending an hour with Amanda is a lucky person indeed. Not only is she well informed she is the most entertaining person I have ever met. Amanda, you are a unique jewel, and I so admire your innovation. You are my hero as a modern woman.

Patricia (Tish) Fried: Editor — Writing Consultant - Director

Thank you Tish. How would I exist without you as Editor? You are so essential for someone like me who has hundreds of ideas exploding from my brain each day. You help me come out the other end with a product. Yah! Thanks Tish! I am so grateful. And I recommend you highly as an Editor and as a professional woman who cares deeply about her clients.
www.theeditingcompany.com
tish@theeditingcompany.com

Frank Don: Business Coach — Writer — Strategist - Astrologer

Frank says, "Color plays an important role in our lives from birth. Knowledge of the meaning of colors can help everyone become a master artist in the art of living." I'd like to give a shout-out to my lifelong friend Frank Don who has written an insightful spiritual book on the deeper meaning of color ... called Color your World available on Amazon. It is included at the Art and Architecture Library of Yale University and at the Royal College of Art in London. Working with energy systems, Frank sees colors as different frequencies that influence and impact us with the conscious use of color providing a means to make our lives more bright and beautiful.

WATCH FOR OUR NEW PRODUCTS!
www.leighruddfashion.com

A FASHION FORECASTING-ENTERTAINMENT WEB SITE AND YOU TUBE CHANNEL COMING IN JULY 2016

Our goal is to develop a vibrant community of fashion and entertainment enthusiasts dedicated to authentic creativity ... and then to showcase their unique talents.

Contact: meadridgemediallc@gmail.com

Hosted by Leigh Rudd & David Wolfe

The original Fashion Forecasters of IM INTERNATIONAL air their candid interviews about how the Fashion Forecasting industry actually began.

COMING SOON: our new Coloring Book for Grown-Ups ... RETRO ACCESSORIES ... Timeless Trends of accessories to color and relieve stress. And! Fashion ideas for dressing up!

A value-packed Coloring Book of 150 Fashion Images ... so much to color. There are detailed sketches of Jewelry, Hats, Fans, Shoes and some surprises!! Look for further news on: www.leighruddfashion.com

ALSO WATCH FOR UPCOMING PUBLICATIONS:
** COLORING BOOK: <u>Fashion Trends: 1970's in NYC</u>

Jordan Parker leaves London to make her mark on the fashion world of New York City as a Fashion Forecaster.

LEIGH RUDD BIOGRAPHY
Creator - Writer – Producer – Fashion Forecaster

Creating this coloring book and the character **Jordan Parker** has been one of my most fulfilling projects over a lifetime. In the process, I was able to re-live so many amazing experiences.

London has a special place in my heart ... always will. I was born there and also founded IM INTERNATIONAL, the Fashion Forecasting Company in 1968. On a personal note ... for years I was unable to admit I'm multi-racial: Cherokee American Indian on my father's side and Irish on my mother's side. It was too different I guess, but now I'm proud of it. My mom was Irish from the Mangan family; her great uncle was Sir Clarence Mangan, the Irish poet.

And this coloring book is based on the true story about how I became a fashion forecaster quite by accident. Yes, I was born with a natural visionary intuition ... but I has no idea what to do with it. In the beginning I made it up as I went along using my Sixth Sense guidance but questioning myself every day. Luckily I had a bull-headed determination. I knew I wanted to make a statement about women ... and for women. To tell the truth I never believed that women were the so-called underclass. So I just forged ahead like a bull in a china shop. I grew up believing women could do what they set out to do. And I still believe that. Positive beliefs, I feel, are at the basis of our success.

Fashion began for me as a ten-year-old child designing wardrobes for paper dolls. In my spare time (of which there was none)I would also conjure up cutting-edge creations: hair décor out of sequins and braided ribbons; patchwork skirts from thrift shop outfits cut up and patched together; little cocktail hats made of old felt; feathers and brooches; and wool jackets I'd decorate with huge old-fashioned buttons and glitzy trims. Family and friends made fun until they noticed these creations would be featured a year later in some fashion magazine. Well, you get the idea. It was quirky! And it was lonely.

THE START OF IM INTERNATIONAL – FASHION FORECASTING
But 1967 marks the start of my real career in fashion, when I interned for the renowned French designer André Courrèges and had the opportunity to work directly for him in his

design room and showroom. He revolutionized fashion in the early 1960's with his "Space Age" mini-dresses worn with white "go-go" boots. He ruled the fashion scene at the time, so it was a prestigious (and exciting) internship! He gave me the responsibility of showing his designs to his elite English-speaking clients like Jackie Kennedy, Gloria Guinness and the Duchess of Windsor. André didn't speak English and cared deeply about his clients, so he would ask me in French what they were saying to me about his designs. He was shy and always calm and sweet.

The other part of my internship was responsibility for getting his new collection to the French fashion magazines to be photographed. And, believe, me it was total chaos; everyone was in a rush and always upset about something. No one spoke English, so I had to negotiate in French (not my first language). It was challenging but so thrilling I could hardly stand it. It was through Monsieur Courrèges that I began to realize how a designer thinks through a design season. I saw him ponder new ideas, question, wonder, care, and finally come up with award-winning designs. I admired him greatly. He was a humble artist full of grace.

It was only a few months later I began to develop my own team of highly creative young people ... the "IM TEAM". At that time, I was still commuting between Paris and London. But slowly I began to embrace a highly unique group of artists, illustrators, textile designers, journalists and art school students. David Wolfe, gifted fashion illustrator, became the first. And I am proud to say we are still the best of friends.

Gradually the IM International Team grew to twenty-five or more full-time fashion innovators. The company expanded until IM had offices in New York City and London with satellite offices in Tokyo, Los Angeles, South Africa, and Spain. In addition we had a staff of fifty "stringers" and photo-editors around the world. By 1970 we were selling our IM publications in over thirty countries: monthly fashion trend reports, seasonal color reports, newsletters, magazines and audio-visual presentations.

The IM Team traveled the world, vacationed in St. Tropez, Ibiza, and photographed Tokyo on-the-street ... and everywhere we went. We attended celebrity galas and museum openings. We even designed some of the costumes for the original Great Gatsby film but never asked for credit. We were young, full of adventure and didn't always need accolades.

However, it was not all glitz and glamour. We were a business and IM was a company whose job it was to make money for corporations (and for ourselves). We spent hours each week analyzing data: socio-economic graphs; cultural changes; new world trends. Yes … we hit the runways but only to confirm our advanced trends. Actually we worked at least six months ahead of Yves St. Laurent, Karl Lagerfeld, Halston, Ralph Lauren and all other top designers.

The entire process of Fashion forecasting was an operating system I personally developed over time to predict trends years in advance. It involved my sixth sense, research, exploration and in-depth analysis. Everything mattered.

Truthfully our feet never hit the ground. We worked ourselves into a frenzy but enjoyed every minute of every day. There were periods of time when we would travel as a group of thirteen with 25 pieces of luggage … and not sleep for three days. It was a Greek tragedy at times. Totally crazy! Thank God we were all under twenty-five!

I love the Fashion business and have a deep respect for this tough and glamorous multi-billion dollar industry and, for all of my illustrious clients and colleagues. Most of all, I am grateful to my staff of highly talented young people. And now I find myself, once again, gathering a group of uniquely talented people … to introduce new concepts in fashion and entertainment.

For more information on IM and how fashion forecasting actually began with Leigh Rudd and David Wolfe watch for our upcoming TV Channel about Fashion forecasting.

To be filmed and edited by Phil Galati, Blue Cast Productions.
www.bluecastproductions.com
bluecastproductions@gmail.com